GALAXY OF SUPERSTARS

Leonardo DiCaprio

Hanson

LeAnn Rimes

Spice Girls

Jonathan Taylor Thomas

Venus Williams

CHELSEA HOUSE PUBLISHERS

GALAXY OF SUPERSTARS

Hanson

Phelan Powell

CHELSEA HOUSE PUBLISHERS
Philadelphia

Produced by
21st Century Publishing and Communications
a division of Tiger & Dragon International, Corp.
New York, New York
http://www.21cpc.com

Editor: Elaine Andrews
Picture Researcher: Hong Xiao
Electronic Composition and Production: Bill Kannar
Design and Art Direction: Irving S. Berman

CHELSEA HOUSE PUBLISHERS

Editor in Chief: Stephen Reginald
Managing Editor: James D. Gallagher
Production Manager: Pamela Loos
Art Director: Sara Davis
Director of Photography: Judy L. Hasday
Senior Production Editor: Lisa Chippendale
Publishing Coordinator: James McAvoy
Cover Illustration: Brian Wible

Front Cover Photo: Kevin Mazur/London Features International, Ltd.
Back Cover Photo: AP/Wide World Photos

The Chelsea House World Wide Web site address is
http://www.chelseahouse.com

First Printing

1 3 5 7 9 8 6 4 2

Library of Congress Cataloging-in-Publication Data

Powell, Phelan.
  Hanson/ Phelan Powell.
  p. cm. – (Galaxy of superstars)
  Includes bibliographical references and index.
  Summary: Examines the history and phenomenal success of the band
Hanson, made up of the three brothers. Isaac, Taylor, and Zach.
  ISBN 0-7910-5148-X (hc)
  1. Hanson (Musical group)—Juvenile literature. 2. Rock musicians—
United States—Biography—Juvenile literature.
[1. Hanson (Musical group) 2. Musicians. 3. Rock groups.]
I. Title. II. Series.
ML3930.H28P69 1998
782.45166'092'2—dc21
[B]   98-42804
                                                                          CIP
                                                                     AC MN

CONTENTS

CHAPTER 1
METEOR SHOWER   7

CHAPTER 2
AT HOME IN OKLAHOMA   15

CHAPTER 3
BOOMERANG
YOU GET BACK WHAT YOU GIVE   25

CHAPTER 4
IKE, TAYLOR, AND ZAC   31

CHAPTER 5
HITTING IT BIG   45

CHAPTER 6
LOOK OUT WORLD! HERE WE COME!   51

CHRONOLOGY   61
ACCOMPLISHMENTS   62
FURTHER READING   63
INDEX   64

METEOR SHOWER

In the spring of 1997, the music world was taken by storm with the meteoric rise of the pop group Hanson. But the three brothers from Tulsa, Oklahoma—Isaac, Taylor, and Zachary Hanson, who formed the band—did not understand the real power of their influence until one day in early May.

Already, Hanson's first hit single, "MMMBop," had been made into a video that aired on MTV, the popular music-video channel, in March. The group had taped a live performance of the song for *The Jenny McCarthy Show* on MTV in February. The boys had fun with the taping because the studio audience did not know who they were. The era of alternative and grunge styles of music led the viewers to believe that Hanson was that kind of band. Isaac, Taylor, and Zachary decided to enjoy themselves by interacting with the audience between camera takes. Their buoyant personalities and fresh good looks won over the audience.

In early May, Hanson was in the middle of a promotional tour before the release of their first major label album, the *Middle of Nowhere*. The band's record company, Mercury Records, had sent the boys to New York City to give the

---

With what has been called a "rare combination of talents," Ike, Taylor, and Zac (left to right) practice their vocalizing. Hanson is known for its superb harmonizing, a talent the boys acquired as young children.

group wider exposure to more people. The brothers shot photo sessions, were set up for television appearances, and answered scores of questions for magazine interviewers.

In the middle of this hectic schedule, a Mercury radio-production executive asked Hanson to cross the Hudson River to Paramus, New Jersey. A local Top 40 radio station, Z-100, had organized a promotion for the band. Hanson was supposed to play a couple of songs on a makeshift stage set up in the Paramus Park Mall. The station told Hanson fans that the band would have a question-and-answer session. Hanson did not think much of the plan. The boys were more interested in continuing their rehearsal for an appearance on *The Late Show with David Letterman*. Nevertheless, they piled into their van and headed across the river.

As the Hanson van neared the parking lot at the mall, the boys were amazed at the crowd of people and cars. Isaac, who likes to be called Ike, said his brothers and he joked about the reason for such a large throng of people. They thought the Sears store was having a sale and that the whole town was coming to participate.

The boys had thought that only a couple of hundred fans would show up for their appearance. When they got to the mall entrance, a mall worker came up to the van and said there was a problem. Approximately 6,000 people were desperately awaiting the band's arrival. Hanson had never played for such a huge crowd. Adoring fans were everywhere. The noise level was terrific, with all the shouting, screaming, and stomping of feet.

Hanson had to make their way from a backstage area to a small platform 20 yards

The brothers help open festivities at the Arthur Ashe tennis stadium in New York in 1997. Along with Ike's guitar, Zac is armed with shakers, and Taylor swings a tambourine.

away. A sea of excited and happy people crowded between the trio and the stage, and security guards had to help the boys push through the masses. The band played two songs, but their music could hardly be heard over the shouts of the fans who had waited for hours to see and hear the new pop sensation. "We would plug our ears and even then the shrieks would cut through," said Taylor, the middle brother. "We were just trying to find a way to block out the pain."

Those who were not screaming sang along with the chorus line of the hit song "MMMBop."

Mmm bop, ba duba dop,
Ba du bop, ba duba dop,
Ba du bop, ba duba dop,
Ba du.

The stage was low and cramped, so no barriers or height separated Isaac, Taylor, and Zachary from the mass of people gathered in the Paramus mall. The band played "Madeline," and the boys were wide-eyed as they watched the excited crowd only three feet away from them. It was pretty heady stuff for three boys only 16, 13, and 11 years of age.

It was decided that it would be impossible to hold the planned question-and-answer session with such a mob. After the two songs, the boys attempted to leave through the shoving, pushing crowd. Family members, some record people, and a few security guards helped protect Hanson from their nearly hysterical well-wishers. Little Zachary was almost swallowed up by the crowd when he tripped on some stairs.

As the van tried to leave the parking lot, fans followed and pushed against the vehicle. In the excitement of the moment, scores of hands pounded out their love on the sides of the van. Ike thought it sounded like so many pellets of hail. "That was pretty cool," he exclaimed.

In the end, however, they all made it through that exhilarating experience. With the appearance at Paramus, Hanson realized they had gotten their fans to love their music as much as they do.

When the "MMMBop" single was released to the public at the beginning of 1997, it started at number 43 on the *Billboard* charts, which measure how many times a song is played on radio stations throughout the country. By the beginning of that summer, the record was number one on the charts, and kids and older folks throughout America, and the world, were

Hanson performances evoke rousing responses from their audiences. Yelling and waving fans often sing along with the band, sometimes even drowning out the boys' music.

expressing themselves with its carefree chorus line that began, "MMM bop, ba duba dop . . ."

Shortly after their Paramus performance, Hanson was highlighted in an *Entertainment Weekly* article of May 9, which described the band as a fresh reaction to the "tormented grunge brats" who seem "freakishly mature for their age" as they belt out "inordinately angst-ridden and world-weary" tunes. The article noted that the 11-, 13-, and 16-year-old trio sounds "11, 13, and 16." It went on to say that "'MMMBop' is an undeniable confection. It's a giddy trampoline bounce of a record that tells us to 'hold on to the ones who really care' because in an mmm-bop they're gone." *Entertainment Weekly* compared lead-singer Taylor Hanson's voice to "a squeaky pre-high school Michael Jackson," and described the band itself as a more relaxed version of the Partridge Family. "Hanson," the article declared, "dispenses their share of lame Hallmark profundities, but they primarily sing of what they know about: a broken heart ["Madeline"]; coping with a cookie-cutter world ["Weird"]; the classmate who vanished ["Yearbook"]; and that homeless dude at the bus stop ["Man from Milwaukee" {Garage Mix}]." *Seventeen* magazine, in an August 1997 article, wrote that the Hanson CD *Middle of Nowhere* is a brand of "soulful pop" that is "fun, relaxed and totally infectious, and provides the perfect antidote to '90's angst."

For Hanson, it has seemed like a lifetime ago since they first learned to harmonize while singing grace at the family table. So much has happened from the time the brothers traveled

around their hometown of Tulsa, singing a capella (without accompaniment) at small neighborhood functions. It has been quite a while since the three last went up to a stranger and asked, "Can we sing for you?"

Never in their wildest dreams could the boys imagine that young girls the world over would display Hanson posters on their walls or that adults of all ages would appreciate their snappy, fresh repertoire as well as their clean performances and reputations. It has all happened, however, and it is all good. At the brothers' young ages, only the sky is the limit for Hanson.

Trying to get a glimpse of their idols, a crush of teens waits for a Hanson performance. The boys still remain awed by the adulation of their fans.

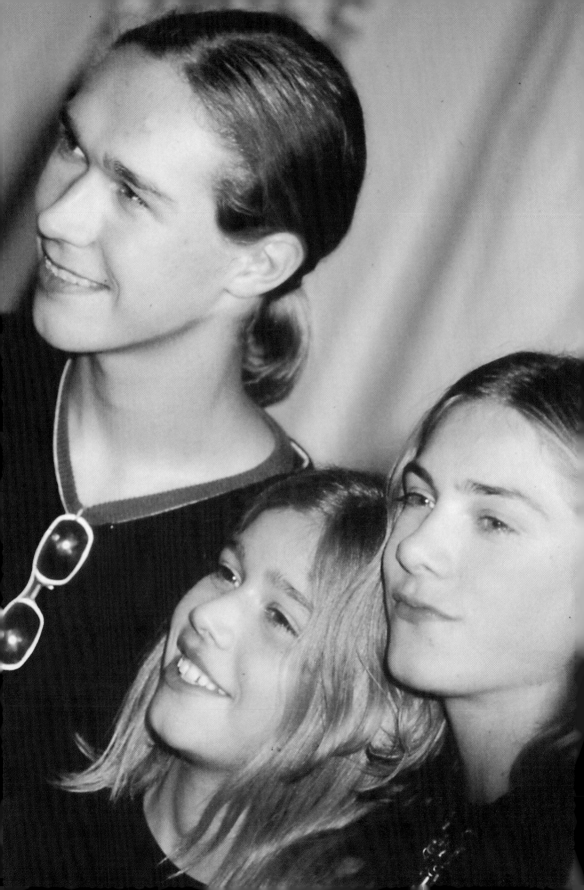

2

AT HOME IN OKLAHOMA

Isaac, Taylor, and Zachary Hanson grew up with a love of the music and singing that they had heard in their home since birth. The boys are Tulsa born and bred, as are their parents, Walker and Diana, and great-grandparents. Walker and Diana, who attended the same high school, were both heavily involved in music. Diana majored in music in college, and Walker played guitar. They acted and sang in many plays and eventually toured with a Christian singing group called the Horizons. The group's singing schedule took Walker and Diana to performances in churches around the country. Eventually, the couple married, and Walker took a job with one of Tulsa's oil-drilling companies.

The couple's firstborn, Isaac, came into the world on November 17, 1980. He was christened Clarke Isaac, but even as a blond, brown-eyed baby, he was called "Ike." Taylor, who is fondly called "Tay," was born on March 14, 1983. Although blond like his older brother, his eyes are a sparkling blue. The youngest member of the group is Zachary, "Zac," who arrived on the scene October 22, 1985.

From their beginnings in Tulsa, the Hanson brothers have retained the clean good looks and natural charm that has captivated audiences around the world. Their image is not an act but a genuine reflection of their upbringing and lifestyle.

Zac, who soon became known as the most energetic of the three, has an infectious smile that shines under his brown eyes and mane of blond hair.

In their early years, the three often heard their mother and father singing little songs they had made up, and both parents sang lullabies to their young sons at bedtime. The singer Billy Joel was one of Diana's favorites. The boys listened to music on the radio and liked to sing along.

When the children were old enough to sit around the dinner table, Diana and Walker realized the three had something special when they harmonized the "Amen" after saying grace. The brothers enjoyed singing it as much as Diana and Walker enjoyed hearing it. Soon the three started to create their own songs and worked hard at making their harmony sound really special. Ike, Tay, and Zac enjoyed singing so much that they often harmonized together instead of playing outside or watching TV.

By the time Ike was old enough for school, his parents had already decided it would be best for their children to be schooled at home. Home schooling has become more and more popular throughout the country over the last 10 years. By the mid and late 1980s, many of Tulsa's children were being taught by their parents at home.

As it turned out, home schooling made life easier when a major change occurred in the Hanson household. In the late 1980s, Walker's company told him he would have to work overseas for a year. He would be required to travel to several different countries during that time. One of the most traumatic events in a child's

Although Tulsa is known for its oil refineries, the city has been the home of many musicians and songwriters. The boys' musical parents encouraged them to develop their talents, helping the brothers to become among the most famous of the city's musicians.

life is to be uprooted from a familiar school and forced to start out new in some strange place. Ike, Taylor, and Zac did not have to worry, however. Their school was wherever their home was located. The brothers were going to spend the next year in South America and the Caribbean, living in Ecuador, Venezuela, and the islands of Trinidad and Tobago.

Before the Hansons packed their bags for their big adventure, Diana and Walker told their sons that one part of their lives would be very different. The music the boys were used to hearing would not be broadcast on foreign radio stations. Diana had a good idea, however. In an interview with *Tulsa World* magazine, Ike explained how his mother solved the problem.

"Before we left, we bought a bunch of tapes, the Time/Life compilation series of old '50s and '60s rock 'n roll—everything from 1957-1969. We had no radio to listen to and it was just a coincidence that we picked this particular style to take with us. But it was very inspirational. It's just great music, all that Chuck Berry, old Beatles, Bobby Darin, Otis Redding, and Aretha Franklin. These people are the origins for what all music is today. They're the ones who started it all. We love that kind of music." Says Taylor, "There's really nothing like that music. Those guys are our heroes."

It was a miracle that the tapes were not worn out, since the brothers listened to them so often. In addition, Walker also conducted family sing-alongs each night to get everyone happily harmonizing together. The family's songfests went a long way toward improving some of the downside of living in such unfamiliar places. Gone were the malls, TVs, and cars to which American families are so accustomed.

The Hansons lived in oil camps often located in the middle of a forest. The sounds of the night were entirely unlike what they were familiar with back in Oklahoma. It was not unusual for the boys to see crocodiles slipping through the water or to watch brightly colored parrots flying by. The family enjoyed the warmth of the South American and Caribbean climates, however. And when they were not with the friends they had made with other oil-company families, they were together, singing and dancing to such tunes as "Splish Splash" and "Good Golly Miss Molly."

It was while they were away from home that the boys first started to write their own songs. Ike, being the oldest, tried his hand at it first. Struck by the poor people he saw in Ecuador, he wanted to write a song about his feelings. The family had brought a small electric keyboard with them, and Taylor had his mother show him some chords on the instrument so that he could accompany his brother. Soon the boys were writing other songs—from their daily experiences with friends and family to love songs. To keep their music from being forgotten, they taped their songs on cassettes.

Before their year abroad was up, Ike, Tay, and Zac were presented with a little sister, Jessica, who was born in 1988. The following year, the Hansons returned home to Tulsa and their family and friends. Another sister, Avery, was born in 1991. Zac was no longer the youngest boy when Mackenzie, the family's sixth child, was born.

A busy, happy place, the Hanson household was full of songs, love, and laughter, as well as chores to be done, including washing dishes. Sometimes, however, tasks were neglected. Diana and Walker often returned home after an evening out to find the kitchen sink still full of dirty dishes. "Instead of doing our chores, we usually spent the time writing a new song," Zac explains. Diana and Walker were not terribly upset, however. They were willing to lend a listening ear to the boys' new creation; then they made the brothers do the dishes.

When Diana decided that the boys needed some formal music training, Ike began taking piano lessons, which he continued for five years. Both Taylor and Zac followed in his footsteps. All three boys took to the piano easily.

Until the end of 1991, when Ike was 11, Taylor was eight, and Zac was six, the boys had not performed for anyone but themselves and their parents. Then, in December, Walker's company held a Christmas party for its employees. In the middle of the festivities, the boys suddenly decided they wanted to entertain the crowd, and they began singing a cappella with no instruments and no music; the three just snapped their fingers and harmonized together. When the delighted partygoers broke into cheers for the trio, that was it! The brothers now knew what they wanted in life—more of the appreciation that a roomful of people will give when they have thoroughly enjoyed what they have heard and seen.

As 1992 began, the boys decided to call themselves the Hanson Brothers, and they started performing at various events throughout their community. Usually they did not get paid but sang for the love of it—at barbecues, parties, and family reunions. The young trio looked a bit different from the way audiences see them today. Their hair was shorter, and they sometimes dressed alike. They might wear matching Hawaiian shirts at one event or denim jackets another time. Often they wore sunglasses to complement their blond hair.

One of the brothers' first big performances

was at the NAIA Men's National Basketball Championship, held every year in Tulsa, to which the boys were invited to sing during half-time. Their next major gig was in May 1992 at the annual Tulsa music and arts festival called Mayfest. Many popular professional musicians performed during this week-long spring celebration, where a spot was reserved for local aspiring performers to show off their music. Taking advantage of the opportunity, the Hanson Brothers sang 15 songs, six of which they had written themselves, during an hour-long performance. Walker told an interviewer later that "Isaac and Taylor really worked off each other well, and Zac picked up the rhythm."

Fans and bands converge at the South by Southwest conference in Austin, Texas, where the boys made the rounds of record company people, singing a cappella and hoping for auditions.

Because they wanted to jazz up their performances, the boys began taking dance lessons. They had definite ideas about how they wanted to present themselves at that time. "We want to be a Boyz II Men/Ace of Base type group where we can sing harmony and dance," Ike told an interviewer from *Urban Tulsa* magazine.

Promotion through word of mouth began paying off for the trio. Eventually they traveled out of state to perform in Louisiana and Missouri. Between taking care of studies and traveling to their gigs, the Hanson Brothers' schedule was practice, practice, practice.

Just as Diana and Walker took care of the boys' schooling, they also decided to be the brothers' road managers. Because bookings were coming in fast and furious, Diana took charge of making all arrangements. Drawing up a long list of all the people she knew had seen the boys perform, she sent out notices of when and where the brothers would next perform.

By 1993 the brothers became known simply as "Hanson." Ike, Taylor, and Zac were getting their first taste of fan adoration as they performed at local schools. Girls often screamed out their favorite Hanson brother's name when the boys appeared on stage. Some in the audience even asked for autographs. The boys loved the attention, but the squeals and shrieks often kept them from talking to their excited fans.

The more appearances the Hanson brothers made, however, the more they wanted to perform.

In the spring of 1994, the family traveled to a major music conference, the South by Southwest, in Austin, Texas. The conference attracted thousands of musicians who were hoping to be seen by the hundreds of record-company people in attendance.

"We got there the last day," said Taylor to a reporter. "There was an outdoor barbecue going on and all these industry people were there. We would just walk up to them and say, 'Can we sing for you?' Some of them would just push us away and say 'Sorry,' and some of them listened, but just kind of blew us off." The boys were entering the rough and tough world of the music business. Even though they were discouraged, they were not going to let the rejections get them down. They kept on keeping on.

3

BOOMERANG
YOU GET BACK WHAT YOU GIVE

At one point during the Austin conference, the Hanson brothers approached an entertainment lawyer, Christopher Sabec, who represented the Dave Matthews Band at the time. Sabec was looking for some new and different talent, but he was not sure what that talent would be. When the brothers sang and danced for him, Sabec was immediately impressed and asked the boys if he could speak to their parents. Sabec left the conference the next day, but he took the Hanson's telephone number with him.

The brothers returned home without a record contract but with an ever-growing following of fans, most of whom were elementary-school-age students. After a Hanson brothers' performance, these enthusiastic kids were able catch their breaths just long enough to ask for autographs—and CDs. The boys knew what was important to do next: they had to record.

By 1994, Ike, Taylor, and Zac had a large collection of material, both classic pop tunes as well as more than 50 original songs. Now was the time to enlist their parents' help in finding and paying for studio time. Since the boys were not playing instruments at this time, they hired studio

Without instruments and just snapping their fingers, the boys create the right beat as they harmonize. For their first CD, Boomerang, *they used backup music because they had not yet mastered their instruments to play as a band.*

musicians and two producers to help them create a polished product. The first CD they recorded, in the fall of 1994, was *Boomerang.* Although *Boomerang* was not given any radio time, the trio promoted their music by selling the CD along with Hansons' T-shirts after each of their performances. Record stores in Tulsa also agreed to sell the items.

The brothers did send *Boomerang* to numerous record companies in the hope that the CD would result in a contract. To their disappointment, not one company showed any interest. "Record companies were afraid to sign us [on the basis of *Boomerang*]," Taylor told a reporter, "because we're white kids doing R&B music, and it didn't exactly work."

Never ones to let rejection overcome them, Ike, Taylor, and Zac planned their next course of action. They realized that now it was time to expand their talent by taking up instruments and becoming a band. But the Hansons did not rush out and buy top-of-the-line, new equipment from a local music store. Instead, Ike, who had decided to take up the guitar, his father's favorite instrument, bought one at a pawn shop; Taylor borrowed some keyboards from a friend; Zac got a set of drums from a friend's attic. The boys admit that at first they were not all that good. They were so committed to becoming a band and not just a singing group, however, that they practiced constantly. The family living room, already rearranged so that the brothers could practice their dance routines, became the band's main rehearsal area.

The Hanson roller-coaster ride soared further into the commercial arena when the boys shot a video of themselves in the fall of 1995 and used it to audition for a soft-drink commercial. The brothers landed the job and flew to Los Angeles for filming. Although the commercial was not shown, the video gave record companies a chance to see the boys perform. Interest was mounting, and Ike, Taylor, and Zac produced their second CD, *MMMBop.*

By now the Hansons were becoming more familiar with the rigors of professional recording, and they loved the challenge. "We composed all the songs and played pretty much every instrument," Ike said of the *MMMBop* CD in an interview with *Urban Tulsa* magazine, "except for the bass." Taylor added, "This time we did much more of a pop rock thing, because we were more of a pop rock group, now that we were playing instruments. There wasn't a lot of synth[esized] stuff on it. We completely wrote it."

The boys' popularity had become almost legendary in the Tulsa area. They regularly played at elementary schools, and their young fans swarmed around the trio at the end of each performance, begging for autographs. The Hansons presented free T-shirts to their young audiences, but school rules forbid them from selling their CD *Boomerang* in the schools. The brothers took orders, however, and personally delivered the CDs.

Many people in the Tulsa area were beginning to realize that the Hanson brothers were appealing to a much wider audience than just elementary-school students. The trio's clean sound, fresh-scrubbed looks, and infectious personalities delighted adults as well. As their manager, their mother saw an opportunity to widen the boys' appeal through the help of a

Preteen and teenage girls are among Hanson's most avid fans. They greet each performance with near-hysterical excitement.

friend who owned the Blue Rose Café in Tulsa. The cafe was a blues/rock club whose bar catered to adult music fans. Diana approached the owner, Tom Dittus, with the idea that her boys should play there. There was a problem, however. State laws throughout the country forbid minors to enter places that serve alcohol. Thinking it over, Tom Dittus came up with a way the boys could be heard in his cafe. They could play in the adjacent parking lot while adult customers on the club's deck could enjoy their music. Underage kids could and did crowd into the parking lot, cheering their approval as the boys played. Ike, Taylor, and Zac performed several times at the club, gaining an ever-widening circle of fans.

In 1996 the Hansons once again performed at the Mayfest in Tulsa. This time the *MMMBop* CD was available, and the fans went wild over it. After enjoying a great performance by the brothers, the audience was happy to take the brothers' music home with them.

Meanwhile, Christopher Sabec, the entertainment lawyer who had heard the boys in 1994 at the Austin conference, was shopping the music industry for a record deal. Record companies throughout the country try to predict where music trends will go. They often jump on new and fresh music before the listening public even realizes it will be turning to a new sound. Many in the industry felt that the alternative and grunge styles of music had already reached their peak and would be less popular in the future. The industry was predicting that most people had become tired of songs about depressed and angry people.

For the Hansons, the break came when Sabec was finally successful in getting their music into the hands of Steve Greenberg, a Mercury Record Company executive. Greenberg heard the Hanson sound, and he was excited. He was also worried, however. "I got this tape and I loved it—but I was convinced it was a fake. I thought maybe they had been manufactured," he told an interviewer with *The New York Times*. "I was sure there was some adult pulling the strings, or the vocals were manipulated, or they were not really playing their instruments."

In the past, record companies had fallen for groups that quickly rose to the top only to fall just as quickly when the public realized the performers were not actually singing their own songs or playing their own instruments. Greenberg did not want to make that mistake. But Hanson sounded so good to him that he agreed to see and hear for himself. Invited by Christopher Sabec, Greenberg attended a Hanson performance at a fair in Coffeyville, Kansas, where the boys were playing. It was April 1996, and the Hansons already had several hundred live performances under their belt.

Taylor was not happy with the show that Greenberg attended. He did not feel it was one of the trio's better-performed or better-attended performances. But after the show Greenberg and Sabec met with the boys and talked with them and their parents far into the night. Greenberg saw what he needed to see: three young musicians who were real, talented, and very personable. He loved the Hansons! Within a few months, Mercury was ready to take them on.

IKE, TAYLOR, AND ZAC

Just who are these three boys who have made such a mark in the music world in such a short time? You can not really say they are just your average neighborhood kids. Although they could blend in with any group of young people anywhere, their personal drive, ambition, and talents place them far above the norm. These boys grew up with a dream and have had the energy, strength, and focus to work hard to make it become real. Even though the boys blend together to create an outstanding team called Hanson, as in any family, each has his own special character, likes, and dislikes.

Ike

Ike, the oldest, is usually known as the serious and moody brother. It is not, however, a negative trait that drives him into teenage angst. He, like most firstborn children, knows what he likes and sticks to it. "We were always doing the kind of music we love to do," Ike told *MTV News* in an interview. "We weren't worrying about what other bands were doing. We do what we do. And they do what they do. Besides, there's enough hard stuff in life,

---

Taylor, Zac, and Ike are more than brothers. They are kindred spirits whose give and take have created fresh musical ideas and appealing, catchy melodies.

plenty of stuff to get us down. For us, our music is a way to get away from things."

No matter what a person does, some critics are always around who have something to say about it. Hanson has been criticized for their music, their long hair, the way they dress. But Ike, who is five-foot-ten and still growing, does not care. His belief in himself and his music cuts right through any negative comments he might hear or read. "Some people make fun of Hanson," he says, "but I don't give a rip."

At 18, Ike considers himself just a regular guy. He is at the junior level in high school, but he and the other children are still taught at home. Diana's decision to school her children at home has worked out well given the busy schedule of the boys' music careers. It would have been extremely difficult to meet state standards for attendance if the boys had been enrolled in public school. Home schooling requires a great deal of discipline and commitment on both the parents' and children's part, and the Hanson family has both. Many people think one downside of home schooling is the lack of social life for the student. That certainly is not the case with Hanson. The brothers have the ultimate social life, playing for and being loved by thousands of fans a month.

Ike says a big advantage of home schooling is that the brothers get to see things and places they study about. "I think it's really neat to read about history-type stuff," he told a reporter from Tulsa. "We were reading about Winston Churchill when we were in England. History is cool when we're on tour, and in Europe we got to see all the things we normally only read about."

Ike, the "serious" brother, began making up songs when he was in the third grade. He was determined at an early age that songwriting and singing would be his career.

Ike is a serious young man, but he also can be quite a cutup. He likes to clown around by imitating such cartoon characters as Beavis and Butthead. Although he tries to make sure his brothers do not goof off too much during rehearsals, often he will break up a moment with a silly cartoon voice. One of Ike's responsibilities is to see that the brothers have all their equipment on hand for each rehearsal and performance. His leadership role comes naturally to him, and he feels very protective of all his younger brothers and sisters. Ike is especially protective of Jessica, Avery, and Mackenzie, who are not as yet involved in the Hanson music machine. When he is asked if the younger ones will be part of Hanson, Ike says firmly it is important that the younger three members of the family do what they want to do. He stresses that his mother and father were never typical stage parents. They always made it clear that if the three brothers wanted to abandon their music performances, it would be fine with them. Diana and Walker never pushed the boys into performing but offered any help they could give to get the boys where they wanted to be. Ike appreciates all the sacrifices his parents have made to help the band pursue their dreams.

Ike has been composing songs since he was in the third grade, writing both the words and the music. Thanks to the piano lessons he began at age five, he was able to read and write the notes. He remembers how much he enjoyed singing and writing at that age, even though he did not have the slightest idea where it might lead. Ike did it for the pleasure it gave him.

When the boys sang for the first time at their dad's company Christmas party, Ike got a bonus. He realized that he could do something he loved—writing and singing—and people would applaud him for it. It was a great feeling to have an audience show how much they liked him and his brothers. Ike never looked back after that. He knew what he wanted to do with his life no matter what it took to accomplish his goals.

Starting out, Ike loved performing the '50s' and '60s' music Hanson was first known for. The songs were engraved on the trio's hearts from all the time they spent listening to the music while living overseas. The happy, catchy tunes set the tone for the light, zippy music style Hanson adopted.

Ike is especially proud of the success of "MMMBop," the single that became a number-one hit throughout the world. The strange thing, Ike says, is that it was never meant to be a song. "We started it in 1994. It was supposed to be a background part for one of the songs we were writing for *Boomerang.*" It was that background piece of music which skyrocketed Hanson from its local performances onto the world stage. The brilliance of "MMMBop," which means "a moment of time," lies in the fact that it transcends the language barrier. "MMMBop" sounds the same and means the same in any tongue the world over.

For fun, when he has some free time, Ike likes to do things that kids everywhere do. He loves roller-blading and street hockey, and his favorite foods are pasta and pizza. His favorite movies are those with plenty of action such as

Star Wars, which he likes best. He says he is not much of a fan for romantic films. Ike does not have a girlfriend, since it is not easy to have a serious relationship when he travels so much. But he certainly is attracted to girls, even naming a couple of his guitars after girls he really liked. If you ask what current music Ike enjoys, he will name such performers as the Spin Doctors, Counting Crows, No Doubt, and Garth Brooks. The Spin Doctors have said they have been most influenced by a lot of the '60s' sounds, just as Hanson has. Ike cannot help but like Garth Brooks because Brooks was also born and bred in Ike's hometown of Tulsa.

Some of Ike's other "likes" are the color green, chunky peanut butter, and science-fiction books. He has been working on writing his own sci-fi novel for the past two years. Vanilla ice cream is his favorite. Zac has been known to call Ike "Ikey-Poo" and "Braceface" because Ike wears clear braces. An old brown leather jacket is Ike's favorite article of clothing. Ike is the only Hanson old enough to drive as yet, and even though the trio has made lots of money with their music, he still does not own his dream car, a Corvette. Ike does have a dream girl, however, Cindy Crawford. She can be seen in one of Hanson's videos, *Tulsa, Tokyo and the Middle of Nowhere*. Ike only drinks diet soda because he likes to keep his 135-pound body in the best possible shape. When Ike is too old and too gray to travel the world singing, he will not have any trouble remembering all the wonderful things that have happened in his life. He takes a journal with him wherever he goes.

Taylor

Born Jordan Taylor Hanson, Taylor is the blue-eyed member of the popular trio. He also has the reputation as the most popular Hanson. Known as the shy one, Taylor is more likely to let Ike or Zac do most of the talking when the boys are interviewed. But Taylor is the lead singer on most of their songs, even though all three boys contribute to the vocals.

Taylor also took piano lessons from the age of five, so when the brothers decided to go from a singing group to a band, it was natural for Taylor to grab up the keyboard. He also plays the synthesizer, the bongos, and conga drums. Taylor remembers the first week the brothers performed after getting their instruments. "Put it this way, we got the drums and instruments, and a week later we played live. But that doesn't mean we weren't good when we played live. It just means we got out there and did it," Taylor said. Taylor's comment is a perfect example of the drive and focus Hanson has always had. The boys knew what they wanted and they went after it. If they made a mistake, they would not let it get them down. They simply learned from it and went on.

This is the same approach Taylor and his brother took with their songwriting, too. "We did not even think about it." Taylor explained. "It just happened. There's really no way to predict how you are going to write a song. I would say it's usually music first, because the music is what is inspiring you. A lot of times we just jam, and suddenly the song will be there."

Like his older brother, Ike, Taylor has said he does not have one special girlfriend. But he

When the boys decided to become a band, Taylor took up the keyboard and conga drums, both of which he plays with equal enthusiasm.

does have a major crush on actress Jennifer Aniston. Even though Taylor is shy, he does like to flirt with girls. He feels, however, that his fans would not like it if he were taken with one certain girl. "Fans don't like it [when you have a girlfriend]," he said in an interview with *16 Magazine.* "It's pretty weird. You have a fan asking you for your autograph, and you tell her you have a girlfriend, and it's like 'Oh, bummer.'" Another real reason for not dating someone special, says Taylor, is he just does not have the time. The hectic schedule of a rock band on tour would not likely make for a very serious relationship. There is no doubt about how Taylor feels about girls though. He likes them to be honest and open with him. "I like girls," he says, "but I haven't seen a girl that I can really just go up to without her going, 'Oh, my God! Oh, my God!'"

Taylor realizes that it might be difficult to date a fan; he does not say it would be impossible, however. "If somebody's obsessed with you, it would be kind of hard to go out with her," he says, "You'd take her hand and she'd scream! But if she was nice enough, then, yeah, I'd date a fan."

Instead of dating on his off hours, Taylor likes to curl up with a good book. Classic adventure stories that have good plots and are packed with action are among his favorites. Out of doors, Taylor loves in-line skating, like his brother, Ike, and also enjoys playing basketball and soccer.

Taylor really favors jelly beans. Once fans around the world found this out, he was overwhelmed with the candy his fans sent him, hoping to win his heart. He delights in getting gifts that show someone knows him and is interested in pleasing him. He is still looking for the fan who mailed him her entire stamp collection. Taylor was fascinated by the gift and touched by what it must have meant to its owner, who obviously had taken years to collect the pages and pages of stamps. Unfortunately, the girl did not put her name and address on the gift, so the giver remains a mystery to this day. Taylor is ever grateful for his fans no matter where they are and what they do, and he is often the one of the three brothers to go out of his way to meet and greet a shy admirer.

His favorite drinks are mineral water, Sprite, and root beer, and his two favorite foods are fish and his mom's brownies. Taylor knows what works for him, and one thing that does is wearing blue shirts to complement his beautiful blue eyes. Although it is not noticeable, Taylor has three scars, two on his face and one on his leg, from playing soccer. When he was younger, he also broke his arm falling off his bicycle. "I was going down this huge hill on my bike to see a house my parents thought they might buy. They were driving up the hill as I was coming down, and I saw the car heading toward me," he said of the incident. "I braked, and went straight over the handlebars. I looked at my arm and it had just snapped."

Taylor likes to shop for clothes at the Gap, although he does not buy his size 13 shoes there. While Taylor's feet might not grow much bigger, Hanson's popularity is sure to increase as the years go on. It is no coincidence that Taylor's favorite saying is "Everything changes!"

Zac

It was not long after Zachary Walker Hanson was born that his family realized they had a real ball of energy on their hands. Zac has always been the lively, hyper member of the band. So it is not unusual that until recently his favorite toys were the Power Rangers. Ike and Taylor nicknamed him "Animal," after the crazy puppet who played the drums on the popular Muppet Show. It was a perfect nickname. When the brothers decided to take up musical instruments and form a band, Zac immediately chose the drums. Not one to stand or sit still for more than a couple of minutes, Zac is famous for his goofing around during photo shoots and rehearsals. He is the brother who likes to get the fans going during a performance, and they enthusiastically follow his lead as he urges them to get more into the performance. Zac is also a talented singing member of Hanson and has equal say when the three brothers write their songs.

Hanson has not let their success go to their heads. Like his brothers, Zac has a strong belief in their music, but also like them, he is modest about his abilities. When he was 10, he believed he was not that great a drummer. "But everyone says I can play, so I'll take their word for it." Zac feels the same way as his brothers about Hanson being compared to other groups. Several articles have described Hanson as similar to the Beatles. This astonishes Zac. "The Beatles? I mean, they were the Beatles!" Zac does not feel he and his brothers are actually stars in the world of entertainment. "We think, 'Stars? Where?'" he says.

Always the energetic, hyper member of the trio, young Zac seemed naturally drawn to the drums. He uses them to draw fans into Hanson performances.

Although Zac and his brothers are not boastful about their careers as rock 'n rollers, they do love the opportunities it provides. "The best part is getting the experience and getting to go to the different places. We've already gotten the chance to go to Europe and Japan," Zac says. "We've gotten a great opportunity."

Zac weighs in at less than 100 pounds and has size eight feet on which he puts only Doc Martens. His favorite pastimes are drawing his own comic books and speaking while he is belching. Like most kids his age, he also enjoys playing Laser Quest, Sega, Nintendo, and Sony PlayStation. Zac too likes movies with plenty of action, which is why his two favorite flicks are *Twister* and *Total Recall.*

Since he travels so often worldwide, he can eat at a McDonald's just about anywhere and also catch some pepperoni pizza. Back in Tulsa, however, Zac loves to eat at the restaurant Rex's Boneless Chicken. For dessert, he is most likely to have Jello or chocolate ice cream. One of his hobbies is fairly unusual: he collects miniature shampoo bottles from hotels around the world. At the rate of success Zac and his brothers are experiencing throughout the world, someday he will have to set aside an entire room just to house his collection.

5

HITTING IT BIG

Now that the Mercury Record Company was convinced Hanson was a sound worth promoting, the family got ready to move again. With their parents and brothers and sisters, the boys left their beloved Tulsa to venture to California's Hollywood Hills. Making records is not a hurried business. It would take five long months for the brothers to record their new album, *Middle of Nowhere*.

Hanson was getting more accustomed to having professional musicians involved in their productions. Nevertheless, it was a unique learning experience working with the team Mercury Records had assembled for the boys' new high-powered release. The Dust Brothers and Steve Lironi were hired to work the recording consoles. The highly acclaimed Dust Brothers, John King and Michael Simpson, had produced the big hit *Odelay* with the Beck band as well as an album for the Beastie Boys, while Steve Lironi had worked with some British bands.

From July through November 1996, the boys and a group of professional songwriters, including Cynthia Weil, Barry Mann, Ellen Shipley, Mark Hudson, and Desmond

---

Hanson truly hit the big time when they won the 1997 MTV award for Best Breakthrough and Best Song. Ike smiles approval while Zac and Taylor exult in the honor.

Child, who had worked with Bon Jovi and Aerosmith, perfected their songs. Working with the songwriters was a new experience for the boys, who were long used to doing their own composing. "It was weird at first," said Ike, "because we were learning how to work with other people and learning how to exchange ideas."

The boys knew it would be worth it though. "We were amazed," Taylor said, "that such well-known writers were willing to write with an unknown band on their debut record. A lot of what happens when you're working with other songwriters is you both bring ideas for songs and you work on either one or both your ideas. And sometimes that would make another song come about."

Ike further described the process. "For example, what we were doing with Mark Hudson [who had been a member of the singing Hudson Brothers], really in a lot of ways, was very similar to the way we were used to writing." He went on: "We would sit together in his studio where he has at least twenty-five guitars hanging on his walls. I would grab a guitar, Taylor would go to the B3 organ, we'd set up some drums and we would jam on songs."

The boys could hardly believe where their music had taken them. This was definitely the big-time world of music, and they were thrilled at having the opportunity to work with the Dust Brothers. "They were really cool to work with," said Ike in an interview. "The whole vibe of the studio was very laid back. We'd come to the studio about noon, sit down, and talk a little while and when we felt like starting, we would. They have a great record collection,

obviously, 'cause they use a lot of different sampled things. So they'd play us different records, like 'Three Dog Night' or something by the Pointer Sisters and they have all the Beatles records. It was really cool."

Hanson fully appreciated the talent and experience the music professionals brought to their album. "I think what the Dust Brothers and Steve Lironi kinda brought back to our sound was a little of the R&B—with the loops and scratches and sampled sounds—and combined it with pop-rock," said Taylor. Ike also thought the whole experience was worthwhile.

Although used to composing their own songs, the boys worked happily with other songwriters, working up lyrics, melodies, and arrangements, and finally putting it all together to record.

"We learned a lot," he said, "and we worked a lot." Zac agreed: "Recording an album is tedious. But it's fun. We love to sing, but there's a lot of work involved in making a CD happen."

When the work was done, however, Zac especially enjoyed jumping into the Dust Brothers' pool. "We jumped in with our clothes on!" he said excitedly. Another fond memory of the recording experience was all the wildlife the boys could see from their house. Deer, coyotes, foxes, and large snakes freely roamed the property, which stood within viewing distance of the famous Hollywood sign. "Who knows what wildlife was living in our backyard," said Taylor. "Who would think you could be in the middle of Los Angeles and have coyotes running across your back patio."

When the record company chose the demo songs for the album, Hanson had a group of 15 musicians to help round out their sound. They were truly pleased when they heard the finished product, *Middle of Nowhere.* "There's quite a bit of variety to the songs," the boys expressed. "Some make you want to dance; they're really up and make you feel good. And other ones are really intense; they're like 'Wow, what's this about?' And some are just mellow. We wrote every one and every one has a different meaning for us."

But the boys had been in the music business long enough to know that when *Middle of Nowhere* was released, critics would come out of the woodwork. In an interview with *Billboard* magazine just before the album was released, Taylor said: "People are going to say, 'Oh, they're young kids, they don't play,

they don't write, they were put together, something's got to be screwy about them.' But you have to listen to the album—the music speaks for itself." Ike commented: "I'm sure people will say that we're a novelty act, but we're not and we don't plan to be. It's just their perception of it. Even though being a kid is kind of a carefree sort of thing for the most part, there are definitely a lot of things that stick in kids' minds."

What Mercury Records hoped would stick in kids' minds was the Hanson's third, but most professionally produced album, *Middle of Nowhere*.

Ike, Taylor, and Zac enjoy a relaxing moment in Los Angeles following the release of their album Middle of Nowhere. *The boys recorded so often in the city that it became like a home away from home.*

6

LOOK OUT WORLD! HERE WE COME!

It was great for Hanson to be back home in Tulsa again after their exciting five months in Los Angeles. The boys now had more time for themselves to have some fun, such as hanging out with their friends in between rehearsing for *The Jenny McCarthy Show*. Events did not quite work out that way, however. When a record company spends a lot of money gambling on a new talent, it requires time of the performers. What began in March 1997 was to be a total media blitz throughout the country and the world of the name "Hanson," the boys "Hanson," the music played by "Hanson." Record companies heavily promote their performers in the hope that people will want what they are told is the best music that has ever come along. All this is done so that by the time an album like the *Middle of Nowhere* hits the stores, fans will be lined up by the hundreds to buy it.

Hanson's first task was to shoot a video for the "MMMBop" single. This meant the brothers had to move back to Los Angeles for a while. By now, they had been to Los Angeles so many times that the city really was

The brothers have attracted adoring fans and fame with their concert tours and videos. Here, they take direction from film director Gus Van Sant (Good Will Hunting) for the video Weird, most of which was filmed in New York City's subways.

like a home away from home. The boys did
not find they got as homesick as they once
did. First, Hanson needed to select a director for the video, and they chose Tamra
Davis, who had worked on the Adam Sandler
film *Billy Madison*. She had also directed
videos for Veruca Salt, Luscious Jackson,
and Sonic Youth.

From the beginning, Ike, Taylor, and Zac
were involved in shooting the video, and the
professionals listened to them even as the boys
listened to the ideas of the others. "We brought
up this idea of using shots of the moon," said
Taylor in an interview. "We had thought about
the future and the past. Like 'In an 'MMMBop,'
they're gone,' and you go to the past. . . . 'In an
'MMMBop' they're not there' and you're in the
future on the moon.'" It was a happy coincidence that when the boys told Davis about
their moon idea, she said she had just been
watching some tapes of the old Apollo flights.
The brothers were delighted that they were
developing such a rapport with Davis.

The video was created in just two days. Much
of it was shot in front of what is called a "green
screen." Different backgrounds were projected
onto the screen while the boys sang and played
around. Some other parts were shot in front of a
large cloth flower. Outside shoots showed the
brothers at the beach, roller-blading in a park,
pretending to drive a car, and playing music in
the Dust Brothers' living room.

The *MMMBop* video was released almost
immediately after it was produced. MTV
began to play it right away, and preteens
and teens around the country were eagerly
watching Hanson. In a very short time, the

video shot to the number-one position in the U.S. charts. *Entertainment Weekly* in a June 6, 1997, article proclaimed: "'MMMBop,' the infectious first single from these three fresh-faced Oklahoma siblings, hit number one after only a month in release and is pulling their album, *Middle of Nowhere* (now at number six), along with it." In answer to how Hanson will be spending their summer vacation, the article said, "Watching the charts and shooting a video for their next single, 'Where's the Love.'"

As part of their *Middle of Nowhere* promotional tour, the three brothers appeared on the morning TV program *The Today Show*. They were interviewed by popular anchorwoman Katie Couric before performing "MMMBop" in

Always appreciative of their audiences' loyalty, the boys reach out to greet fans as the trio leaves The Late Show with David Letterman. *Their appearance on the show was just one of several on Hanson's tour to promote* Middle of Nowhere.

front of a live audience. Hanson was also high-lighted on *Live with Regis and Kathie Lee.* Kathie Lee Gifford dreamily complimented the boys' looks by saying they could be surfers. Regis referred to the boys' long hair and remarked, "These guys are a barber's dream." When he asked the brothers if they ever get into squabbles, they laughed and answered that when they were younger they practiced karate on each other. Then Regis mentioned that since the homegrown Tulsa boys had become so famous, the governor of Oklahoma had declared a Hanson Day.

Taylor said, "It's pretty strange."

Kathy Lee asked, "Why not a Hanson Year?"

"I don't know," Taylor responded, "We're pleased with one day."

Within the next couple of weeks, Comedian Jay Leno invited Hanson to *The Tonight Show,* where the boys got to meet its famous host. The brothers performed their hit single "Where's the Love" and then were asked over to Leno's guest couch. Leno wanted to know if the boys were ever asked dumb questions. All three immediately nodded their heads, and Taylor said, "The dumbest question we got asked was 'How did you guys meet?'"

Hanson was impressed with Jay Leno. "Leno is a really nice guy," Ike said later. "He stopped by the dressing room before the show just to say 'Hello.'" Taylor also liked meeting Leno. "He's very down to earth."

It was during that first hectic promotional week that the boys were mobbed in Paramus by 6,000 near-hysterical fans, they knew their lives would never be the same. All the promotional hype paid off. When the *Middle of Nowhere* CD was released, sales reached more than 72,000 during the first week. It started on the charts at number nine, and within a few months it had shot to number two. *Rolling Stone* predicted then that their first single "will stick in your brain like Trident in your shag carpet."

Hanson had long been compared to the Jackson Five and the Partridge Family. While the brothers are emphatic in their belief that their music is unique, they do not mind the comparisons, especially since their music is making them millions of dollars. "I think it's cool when we're compared to groups like the Jackson Five," said Ike in an interview, "because they were amazing. I mean, they were the Jackson Five." Taylor agreed: "They rocked. It's a real compliment when somebody compares us to them. But the way we've always described ourselves is that we're three guys who write, play, and sing our music, and that really pulls it together."

Because the *MMMBop* video was so successful, Hanson decided to work with Tamra Davis again for their next video, *Where's the Love* (from their single), which moans about a relationship that is just not working. The brothers went to England for the filming. Then it was time to go back to the States for another whirlwind tour of four cities.

After hardly catching their breaths back home in Tulsa, Hanson flew to Los Angeles for *The Tonight Show* taping and then left right away for another tour. This time it was to far-off Japan, Southeast Asia, and Australia.

Although Taylor once modestly described Hanson as just "three guys who write, play and sing our music" the band has taken the media by storm, giving interviews, being written up in magazines, and appearing regularly on MTV.

Throngs of enthusiastic fans greeted the boys in Japan. Japanese teens have always been crazy about pop music, and they delighted in Hanson. The brothers kept a hectic schedule with press conferences, interviews, and TV appearances. Throughout Japan, the fans were eager to catch a look at their real-life objects of affection. At one point, so many fans had gathered outside a radio station that the managers decided to give them what they wanted. Ike, Taylor, and Zac sat safely inside a control booth surrounded by glass as they answered questions from the disc jockey. The fans were allowed to come into the station in groups of 20 and walk by the boys.

In Japan, nothing but love was showered on the brothers, and so it was for the next stop on the tour—Australia. The *MMMBop* video was number one on the charts for nine weeks by the time Hanson set foot in the "Land Down Under." Their first stop was the beautiful city of Sydney. For the first time in their professional (and amateur lives), the boys performed on a ship off the shore of Sydney.

"It was kind of an awkward thing," Taylor remembered later, "because we were in the hull of this boat that was packed with a crowd of contest winners. But in that situation it seemed like there were a whole lot more because it was such a small area. Not to mention the video cameras and the press. It was a very unique situation for performing. It's not very often you're on a rocking boat singing to a packed room of girls, after all. It was pretty wild."

"They were definitely very enthusiastic," Ike added. "Before we came down to do the show, all of the crowd were singing 'MMMBop' word for word. I mean they knew every single word." Ike also found the experience different from most of their other performances in front of live audiences. "Before Australia, we'd been doing a lot more concert situations where we were not very close to the audience. But this was different because it was very, very intimate, so it was a lot of fun."

Sydney was not the only place with its Hanson worshipers. The brothers' next stop was Melbourne, Australia's second-largest city. Taylor described what it was like in that city: "After we landed, the flight attendant said, 'You guys need to wait until everybody else gets off the plane. You need to be the last ones off.' We couldn't figure it out and asked 'Why?' They just smiled and said, 'Just wait.' So we waited, and we were the last ones off, and just before we got inside the terminal they said, 'I hope you're ready 'cause there's a lot of people out there.' When we went out into the waiting area it was just totally wacko." Unlike the crowds in Japan, these fans were not controlled. It was definitely what could be called a mob scene.

Everywhere Hanson performed in Australia, it was the same. The boys had scheduled an appearance in a huge shopping mall. When they saw the size of the place before they performed, they were modest enough to think there was no way their fans could fill the space. Little did they realize that 20,000 screaming admirers would turn out to see them in person.

From Australia the brothers went on to Java and the Indonesian capital of Jakarta, where the wildness continued. At the Hard Rock Café, they were supposed to have a question-and-answer session and then sing a couple of songs for a limited audience inside the restaurant. If Hanson fans are one thing, they are determined. The boys had barely gotten through one song when a crowd

At the 1998 Grammy Awards, Ike, Taylor, and Zac get together with a fellow musician, country singer LeAnn Rimes. Although superstars almost overnight, success for Hanson still means singing the best they know how and having fun doing it.

pushed through the doors and spilled into the restaurant. Once inside, the fans moved as one toward the small stage on which the boys were performing. All of a sudden, the security guards started yelling for the boys to get off the stage. "People were just pushing and shoving," Taylor said. "I mean, photographers were going down on the floor. The press was not exactly ready for it."

Eventually, Hanson was able to sing two more songs. When they left, however, the madness continued. "People were grabbing parts of our clothing," Ike recalls. "They were grabbing our hair and pulling it, and jumping on us and almost ripping off our clothes."

After Hanson had finally escaped, the restaurant management had to deal with the fans who would not believe the trio had actually left the building. "They played a video tape of the songs we had just done and we were told that everybody started crying and taking pictures of the video screen," Zac told a journalist. "Definitely an experience to remember."

Hanson had a few more stops in North America before returning to New York City to film a video for their third hit single, "I Will Come to You." The group's tour schedule continues to take them on the road through 1998. During the year they will travel throughout the United States, performing for their ever-adoring fans.

How far can they go after reaching the top? The brothers are philosophical about their success. Ike said, "The funny thing is, all this can go as fast as it came. We're just having fun with it." Taylor is all for the fun part of their young careers. "I think you have to make sure that you're always having fun. Make sure you're doing something you really want to do and then put your whole heart into it." Zac, the youngest, can be thoughtful beyond his years. "We love music and music is really a part of us. But we also would love to do other things too."

One thing is for sure: Whatever these three dynamos do, they will be the best at it.

CHRONOLOGY

1980   Clarke Isaac Hanson is born on November 17 in Tulsa, Oklahoma.

1983   Jordan Taylor Hanson is born on March 14 in Tulsa.

1985   Zachary Walker Hanson is born on October 22 in Tulsa.

1992   Form group Hanson Brothers; debut public performance at NAIA Men's National Basketball Championship; first performance at Mayfest, annual May event in Tulsa.

1993   Begin to use group name Hanson.

1994   Attend South by Southwest, a music conference, in Austin, Texas; meet Christopher Sabec, an entertainment attorney; record first CD, *Boomerang*.

1995   Record second CD, *MMMBop*.

1996   Perform again at Mayfest to a larger audience; meet Steve Greenberg, Mercury Records executive; sign contract with Mercury Records; record third CD, *Middle of Nowhere*.

1997   Tape appearance on *Jenny McCarthy Show*; shoot video *MMMBop* in Los Angeles; *MMMBop* video airs on MTV; "MMMBop" hits number one in the United States and Britain; swamped by 6,000 fans in Paramus, New Jersey; *Middle of Nowhere* CD reaches number-two spot; film *Where's the Love* video in England; shoot *I Will Come to You* video; film video compilation *Tulsa, Tokyo and the Middle of Nowhere*; win MTV European Music Awards for Best Breakthrough and Best Song.

1998   Release *3 Car Garage* album, featuring early versions of Hanson hits; film *Weird* video with director Gus Van Sant; attend and perform at 1998 Grammy Awards.

ACCOMPLISHMENTS

Albums/CDs

    1994 *Boomerang*

    1996 *MMMBop* (demo)

    1997 *Middle of Nowhere* (major label debut)
           Snowed In (Christmas album)

    1998 *3 Car Garage*

Singles

    "MMMBop"

    "Where's the Love"

    "I Will Come to You"

    "Weird"

    "River"

Video

    Tulsa, Tokyo and the Middle of Nowhere (video compilation)

    MMMBop

    Where's the Love

    I Will Come to You

    Weird

Award

    1997 MTV European Music Awards for Best Breakthrough
           and Best Song, November 6.

FURTHER READING

Gollihare, Jarrod. *Hanson.* London: Virgin Books, 1997.

Krulik, Nancy. *Isaac Hanson.* New York: Pocket Books, 1998.

Krulik, Nancy. *Taylor Hanson.* New York: Pocket Books, 1998.

Matthews, Jill. *Hanson.* New York: Pocket Books, 1997.

Netter, Matt. *Zac Hanson.* New York: Pocket Books, 1998.

ABOUT THE AUTHOR

Phelan Powell wrote for her college newspaper in Boston and also created a cartoon strip for the paper. As a journalism student, she wrote feature articles for the University of Maryland *Diamondback.* While serving in the Coast Guard Reserve, Powell worked in the Public Affairs office, dealing with press relations. She was the daily correspondent for the *Michigan City News-Dispatch.* Having completed two titles, books on Tom Cruise and John LeClair, which will be published in 1998–99, Powell is currently working on other books for Chelsea House Publishers.

INDEX

Aerosmith, 46
Aniston, Jennifer, 39
Beastie Boys, 45
Beatles, 18, 41, 47
Berry, Chuck, 18
Billboard, 10, 48
Bon Jovi, 46
Brooks, Garth, 36
Child, Desmond, 45-46
Churchill, Winston, 32
Counting Crows, 36
Couric, Katie, 53
Crawford, Cindy, 36
Darin, Bobby, 18
Dave Matthews Band, 25
Davis, Tamra, 52, 55
Dittus, Tom, 28
Dust Brothers, 45-48, 52
Franklin, Aretha, 18
Gifford, Kathie Lee, 54
Grammy Awards, 59
Greenberg, Steve, 29
Hallmark, 12
Hanson (Hanson
   Brothers)
   awards, 45
   childhood, 15-23
   home schooling, 16-17,
      22, 32
   living overseas, 17-18
   performances, 8-13,
      20-23, 25, 27-29,
      54, 57, 59, 60

promotion tours, 7-8,
   53-60
recording/filming, 25-27,
   45-49, 51-53, 55, 60
songwriting, 19, 37, 41,
   46-47
TV show appearances, 7-8,
   53, 54
Hanson, Avery, 19, 34
Hanson, Clark Isaac (Ike),
   7-10, 15-17, 19-20, 22,
   25-28, 31-37, 45-47, 49,
   52, 54, 56-57, 60
Hanson, Diana, 15-17, 19-20,
   22, 28, 34
Hanson, Jessica, 19, 34
Hanson, Jordan Taylor (Taylor,
   Tay), 7, 9-10, 12, 15-20, 22-
   23, 25-29, 31, 37-40, 45-49,
   52, 54-57, 59-60
Hanson, Mackenzie, 19, 34
Hanson, Walker, 15-19, 22, 34
Hanson, Zachary Walker (Zac),
   7, 9-10, 15-17, 19-20, 22,
   25-28, 31, 37, 41-43, 45,
   48-49, 52, 56, 60
Horizons, 15
Hudson Brothers, 46
Hudson, Mark, 45-46
Jackson Five, 55
Jackson, Michael, 12
Jenny McCarthy Show, 7, 51
Joel, Billy, 16

King, John, 45
*Late Show with David
   Letterman,* 8, 53
Leno, Jay, 54
Lironi, Steve, 45-46
Luscious Jackson, 52
Mann, Barry, 45
Mercury Records, 7-8, 29,
   45, 49
MTV, 7, 31, 45, 52, 56
NAIA Men's National Basketball
   Championship, 21
No Doubt, 36
Partridge Family, 12, 55
Philbin, Regis, 54
Pointer Sisters, 47
Redding, Otis, 18
Rimes, LeAnn, 59
Sabec, Christopher, 25, 28-29
Sandler, Adam, 52
Sears, 8
Shipley, Ellen, 45
Simpson, Michael, 45
Sonic Youth, 52
South by Southwest Music
   Conference, 21, 23
Spin Doctors, 36
Today Show, 53
Tonight Show with Jay Leno,
   54-55
Van Sant, Gus, 51
Veruca Salt, 52
Weil, Cynthia, 45

PHOTO CREDITS:
Kevin Mazur/London Features Int'l, Ltd.: 2, 6, 11, 42, 59; AP/Wide World Photos: 9, 13, 21, 24, 28, 38, 47, 50, 56; Gie Knaeps/London Features Int'l, Ltd.: 14; Stock Photos: 17; Ron Wolfson/London Features Int'l, Ltd.: 30; David Hum/London Features Int'l, Ltd.: 33; Reuters/Jerry Lampen/Archive Photos: 44; Reuters/Marina Chavez/Archive Photos: 49; Dennis Van Tine/UDV/London Features Int'l, Ltd.: 53.